ALL THE POWER RESTS WITH YOU

BOOKS BY SUZANNE STUTMAN

My Other Loneliness: Letters of Thomas Wolfe and Aline Bernstein. Edited, and with an Introduction by Suzanne Stutman. Chapel Hill: University of North Carolina Press, 1983.

Holding on for Heaven: Postcards and Cables of Thomas Wolfe and Aline Bernstein. Edited, and with an Introduction by Suzanne Stutman. Special Publication of the Thomas Wolfe Society, 1985.

The Good Child's River, by Thomas Wolfe. Edited, and with an Introduction by Suzanne Stutman. Chapel Hill: University of North Carolina Press, 1991.

The Party at Jack's, by Thomas Wolfe. Edited, and with an Introduction by Suzanne Stutman and John L. Idol, Jr. Chapel Hill: University of North Carolina Press, 1995.

Broken Feather: A Journey to Healing. By Suzanne Stutman. Manor House Publications, Inc., 1996.

A Passage to England: A Selection. Edited, and with an Introduction by Suzanne Stutman and John L. Idol, Jr. Special Publication of the Thomas Wolfe Society, 1998.

White Feather: A Journey to Peace. By Suzanne Stutman. Manor House Publications, Inc., 2004.

ALL THE POWER RESTS WITH YOU

By

Suzanne Stutman

Manor House Publications, Inc.
Philadelphia, PA

ALL THE POWER RESTS WITH YOU
Copyright © 2005 by Suzanne Stutman

Library of Congress Cataloging-in-Publication Data

Stutman, Suzanne
  All the power rests with you / by Suzanne Stutman.—1st ed.
    p. cm.
ISBN 0-9648261-7-8 (pbk.)
  1. Conduct of life-Juvenile poetry. 2. Emotions-Juvenile poetry. 3. Children's poetry, American. I. Title.

PS3569. T884A79 2005
811'.54—dc22

                                         2005043874

First Edition 2005

Manufactured in the United States of America

To

Fred

Geoffrey, Samantha, Alana, and Rain

A Note To Caregivers

Dear Caregivers:

Your beautiful children will be encouraged by this book to write poetry expressing feelings about their own lives. This is a very important tool to help them to deal not only with their anger, their loss, their frustration, and their loneliness, but also with their happiness and joy.

Kindly give them the opportunity to share some of the poems with you if they so wish. Please respect their privacy and timing. They might not wish to share some of the poems with you. Sometimes it might come up when least expected. This is because it is the right time for them to share.

Listen to your kids. The poems might encourage them to write their feelings down. Perhaps they will start talking openly about them. Again, remember to listen. They have to find meaning within their own lives and your listening attentively will help them do that.

Thank you for your participation. I hope the children will also inspire you to write down your feelings in poetry.

Best wishes,

Sunette Pienaar, Suzanne Stutman, Gene Corbman, Chris Kirchner, Liane Rice, Sorosh Roshan, and Tammy West

Consultants

Christina M. Kirchner, LSW, Executive Director,
Philadelphia Children's Alliance

Gene R. Corbman, M.D. Psychiatrist, Faculty,
Philadelphia Association for Psychoanalysis

Dr. Rev. Sunette Pienaar, General Manager,
Heartbeat, South Africa

Sorosh Roshan, M.D., M.P.H., President,
The International Health Awareness Network

Liane T. Rice, Legal Services Coordinator,
Women Organized Against Rape

Tammy Ann West, LSW, Director of Counseling,
Women Organized Against Rape

ACKNOWLEDGEMENTS

First and foremost, I would like to thank Christina Kirchner, the Executive Director of the Philadelphia Children's Alliance, without whom this book would not have been written in its present form. Chris was totally dedicated to the creation of this book. Her devotion to the children and her belief that I could do what I set out to do, and her faith that this book would indeed serve the children we all love so dearly has sustained me throughout every stage of this project. From the beginning, Chris supported the proposal for this book. She met with me on several occasions and we discussed each poem and the potential impact each work could have upon the children who were its proposed audience. She has taken an active part in every aspect of the creation of this text.

Through Chris Kirchner's recommendation, Liane Rice and Tammy West from Women Organized Against Rape joined my team of consultants. Both Liane and Tammy through WOAR are involved in counseling and support for children and teens who have been victims of trauma and violence. I met with Chris, Tammy, and Liane on several occasions at The Children's Alliance, the offices of WOAR and at various sites around center city Philadelphia as they devoted their lunch hours to pouring over the text, presenting key suggestions which were guided by their expertise, knowledge in the field, and compassion for children. Liane and Tammy provided the activities for children based upon the poems in this book, activities which I feel are like poems themselves in their creativity and sensitivity toward the children they serve. I am so grateful to them both for the opportunity to share many of my poems with children and teens connected with WOAR, and for the valuable insights these vibrant young people shared with me.

Gene Corbman, M.D., has been my friend and muse for many years. His compassion and expertise concerning the truths of the human heart are in my estimation unparalleled. He is a master of language and symbol. I am grateful to him for his devotion to this project, for his contributions to every aspect of this work, and to his unwavering belief in my ability to create the text that was in my heart.

Sorosh Roshan, M.D., has dedicated herself to the cause of human rights for her lifetime. Her brilliance and compassion have been my beacon for all of the years that I have been privileged to work with her in the National Council of Women of the United States, The International Health Awareness Network, The United Nations, and at many locations around the world to which we have traveled together in our quest for peace and human rights. It was my work with Dr. Roshan and the scholarship program IHAN created for Heartbeat that led me to Dr. Sunette Pienaar, the General Manager and Founder of Heartbeat, South Africa.

I was privileged to spend four days with Dr. Sunette Pienaar and the Heartbeat team in the summer of 2004, and during this time was enchanted to meet many of the wonderful children and teens who are part of the Heartbeat program. Heartbeat is an organization which administers to over 5,000 children in South Africa who have been affected/infected by HIV/AIDS. I was so moved by Sunette's devotion to the children, and to her openness and joy for life, and truly honored to have the opportunity to share my interactive poem "All the Power Rests with You," with children who are part of Heartbeat's aftercare program. Dr. Pienaar has reflected upon all of the poems and has given particular insight into issues which would be significant to South African children and teens. Because of her gentle perspective, I have revised and rewritten poems until we felt they would serve all of the children in a supportive, healing, and empowering manner. I am particularly grateful to her for her help in crafting the Note to Care Givers which begins this text.

I thank all of my consultants, for without their expertise and insight I would not have been able to create *All the Power Rests with You.* It is on behalf of the children that all have dedicated themselves with such devotion.

CONTENTS

PART IV: POSITIVE FEELINGS

PART V: THE FUTURE

INTRODUCTION

<u>All the Power Rests with You</u> is a springboard for helping you to use your own creativity and imagination to express yourself through what we call poetry. Can you tell what makes poetry special? Poetry is different because it is an expression through symbolism and metaphor. In other words, through using words in unusual and creative ways, we can follow the heart's path to feelings which may be otherwise unexpressed. We surprise ourselves often through poetry by making connections between thoughts and feelings we might not even know we have.

Poetry helps us to expand the boundaries of thought and even of what we think about the world around us or within us into the unexplored territories of our hearts and souls and perceptions. It is a world of feelings expressed through sound and rhyme and music, through the pattern of words upon a page, words which come from the wellsprings of our inner selves. What I love so very much about poetry is that it is a creation of the beauty of recognition, of awareness, of seeing and responding to the life within us in a way uniquely our own.

The blank pages in this book are there for you to create your own poems. The beauty of reading poetry is that we can experience the world in ways perhaps before unimagined. It is my hope that my poems can inspire you to write your own poems, and in so doing, create your own path and continue your own journey into creativity and awareness.

This book is my gift to you, my expression of love and hope, and my belief that you are special, and indeed, the most beautiful creation of all.

PART I:
ADVENTURES IN WRITING POETRY

My Declaration of Rights

I have the

Right

To be happy.

I have the

Right

To be safe.

I have the

Right

To protect and

Keep

Within my control

My own body.

I have the

Right

Not to be yelled at

Or insulted,

Or ridiculed

For any reason.

I have the

Right

To learn.

I have the

Right

To dream.

I have the

Right

To my own thoughts.

I have the

Right

To be responsible.

I have the

Right

To be respected.

I have the

Right

To be Loved.

I have the

Right

To cherish

Life

And to

Celebrate

The

Divine and miraculous

Gift

Of my

Unique

And

Indomitable

Self.

.

Poetry: Sunshine of the mind

Sunshine

of

the

mind.

Radiant

luminosity.

Moving

beyond

the

shadows

of

my

soul,

until

I

Face

myself,

astonished

and

serene.

And

dare

to

dream.

Sometimes a poem wears a hat

Sometimes a poem wears a hat,
and sometimes it wears shoes.
In fact, you're free to dress it up
in any way you choose.

It's your creation! You cannot fail
in anything you do.
Because your words and thoughts belong
to no one else but you.

Tall as the sky,
Small as a pea,
Big as the world
Your poem can be.

It can sing of your thoughts,
It can dance to your dreams,
You can dress it in hope,
Or whatever seems—right.

It takes flight
From your mind,
From your heart,
From your soul,
With telling the truth
As you see it, your goal.

So go ahead:

Laugh,
Or sing,
Or rap
Or shout,
Or stamp
Or yell

Or rhyme it out.

Make it happy,
Make it sad
Make it ugly,
Make it mad.
Make it lovely,
Make it funny,
Make it silly,
Make it blue—

Just be sure to make it you.

Valentines

Poems

are

like

valentines

we

give

to

ourselves.

Expressions

of

love,

and

the

creative

spirit.

Poems

make

my

heart

sing.

They

connect

me

with

the

music

inside

myself.

They

help

me

to

bring

out

the

pictures

in

me.

They

make

my

heart

smile.

ACTIVITIES FOR PART 1:
ADVENTURES IN WRITING POETRY

My Declaration of Rights
Poetry: Sunshine of the mind
Sometimes a poem wears a hat
Valentines

What does poetry mean to you? If you've ever written a poem before, why did you do it? Are there things you can say in a poem that you have trouble saying in a conversation? When you write poems, are they for you alone, or do you ever imagine someone else reading them? If you've never written a poem before, what made you decide to start?

How would you respond to the following?

I want to write a poem because:

It's easy to write poems about_____, but it's hard to write about _____.

I feel _____ after I write a poem.

Poetry helps me to:

The best thing about poetry is:

I like poems that:

Poetry is meaningful in different ways to different people.

- Try writing a poem about poetry.
- Write a poem where each line begins with the word "Poetry..." or "A poem..." Like this:

    Poetry _____
    Poetry _____
    Poetry _____

A Poem _____

A Poem _____

A Poem _____

- Write a poem that starts "If this poem could change the world..." or "The day after my poem changed the world..." and tell what happened!

- Re-read "Sometimes a poem wears a hat." If that poem could wear a hat, what kind of hat would it wear? Draw the hat. Pick a poem that you've written and draw a hat for your poem.

Some types of poems have rules. Other poems break all the rules! If it sounds good, it is good. The poems you write in this book can be in any style you want. If you would rather write stories, draw, paint, dance, or sing, go right ahead!

Use the following blank pages in any way you want.

PART II:
FEELING SAFE

On a raft in the middle of the sea of myself

If

I

close

my

eyes,

no

one

can

see

me.

If

I

close

my

eyes,

no

one

can

be

me.

I

can

climb

into

my

mind,

and

float

in

the

dark,

like

on

a

raft

which

bobs

gently

in

a

calm

sea.

I

can

climb

into

my

arms

and

legs—

and

travel

to

the

end

of

creation.

I

can

erase

my

self

from

the

whole

world

and

just

be.

Just

me.

My

self.

Under

the

tent,

time

spent

in

floating

down

the

Great

Divide

of

the

Map

of

the

world

of

Me.

A

universe

of

quiet

and

perfection.

Infinitely

safe.

ACTIVITIES FOR PART II:
FEELING SAFE

On a raft in the middle of the sea of myself

Poetry can be very personal. Do you want anyone to read the poems you write in this book? Would it be OK for some people to read your poems and not OK for other people to read them? Some days you might feel like sharing and some days you might not.

If you want your poems to be private, do you have a safe place to put your poetry book? What would happen if someone read your poetry book?

Now let's talk about you. Do you have a safe place, a place where you feel totally comfortable and protected? For some people, their safe place is a real place, like grandma's house or their backyard. A safe place can also be a memory or something you imagined, like being on a raft in the middle of the sea. It's something that makes you happy when you think about it.

- What does your safe place look like? Draw a picture of it.
- Write down 10 words that describe your safe place. Write a poem about your safe place that uses some or all of those words.
- Write your poem down inside the drawing of your safe place or write your poem so that it's the same shape as your safe place.

```
              |F|
              |o|
            _ |r|
            /  E  \
          __/xample,\__
          | if your poem |
          | were a house, |
          | it might look |
          | like this one. |
```

33

PART III:
FEELING OUT OF PLACE

So me times I feel so out of step

So me times I feel

     so stupid
     so different
     so angry
     so lonely
     so tired
     so wired
     so foolish
     so scared
     so abandoned
     so weak
     so ashamed
     so guilty
     so out of step
     so secret
     so bad
     so mad
     so wacky
     so crazy
     so lazy

So me times I feel like I can't move.

I'm outside of time.

I'm out of space.

I'm not in this world.

I'd like to

Erase

myself.

So me times I feel like I just can't make

another day.

Like I can't pray.

Like I could

Tell

on

Everyone.

But then I can't.

So me times I feel

like

a

tiny

ant.

So me times I feel

that

no one can see

any thing I do

they can't see

me.

So me times I feel

that I'm all they see:

      ugly
      dirty
      lost
      alone

Without a family.

Without a home.

Without a language

that can tell

how I feel.

      too old
      too young
      too big
      too small
      too fat
      too thin
      too short
      too tall

I can't fit in

anywhere

anywhere at all.

So me times I feel

in outer space.

I

could

just

Erase

      my face
      my arms
      my legs
      my toes
      my nose

and

just

not

be.

But I can't

I can't

I can't

I won't

e rad I cate

Me.

I want to be somebody from somewhere

Sometimes

 I

feel

like

no body

from

no where.

Nobody

sees

me

and

no one

seems

to

understand

the

things

I

say

or

do.

I

feel

lost

then,

like

I

don't

know

how

to

find

my

way

back

home.

The

door

is

missing.

Inside

myself

is

hard

to

follow

and

I

don't

know

where

to

go.

People

don't

really

hear

me

or

see

me.

I

just

seem

to

be

invisible

to

everyone.

I

want

to

be

Some body

from

Some place.

 I

want

people

to

say

hi

and

smile

and

invite

me

in

to

Every place.

I

want

to

feel

Big

inside

and

open,

like

a

forest

of

tall

trees

that

hug

the

earth

And

reach

Up

to

the

Sky.

I

want

to

say

I

and

have

people

Listen.

Then

I

will

be

Somebody.

Sometimes it's hard to just keep on going

Sometimes

it's

hard

to

just

keep

on

going.

Sometimes

it

feels

like

all

the

cracks

are

showing,

in

the

bottom

of

the

world.

Sometimes I feel like a dog who quacks

Sometimes

I

feel

like

a

dog

who

quacks

or

a

cat

who

moos.

It's

the

con

tra

dic

tory

things

I

do.

As

if

up

was

down,

or

yes

was

no,

or

in

was

out—

you

know

what

I

mean. O O

Sometimes

I

feel

like

a

Mean

machine.

I

don't

say

what

I

think.

I

don't

think

what

I

say.

I

am

up

and

down

in

a

funny

way.

But

it's

not

funny.

I

just

don't

understand

why

I

say

or

do

the

stuff

I

do.

Sometimes

it's

hard

just

being

me.

In

side

it's

tough,

sometimes.

Can anyone see?

Sometimes

things

happen

to

hurt

us

a lot.

Sometimes

we

feel like

we're

bad when we're

not.

Sometimes it feels

like

there's no where

to

go

and

no body

to

listen.

It's almost

as

though

we are

all

alone

in

the

whole

wide

world

with

our

secret

self

and

our

pain

all curled

in

a

tight

small

space

that

is

dark

and

still

and

we

cry

inside

and

we

just

can't

fill

all

the

empty

spaces,

the

sorrow

places.

We

feel

so

alone

and

so

different

then,

Like

we

have

two

heads

or

three

noses.

And

things

that

we

can't

tell

to

Anyone

else,

since

they

wouldn't

believe

Us.

Sometimes,

we

can't

even

believe

what

we're

feeling

ourselves.

We're

so

mad

and

lonely

and

scared

and

sad,

We

feel

ugly

and

dirty

and

awful

and

bad—

like

no

one

can

Love

us

not

even

ourselves.

And

the

world

seems

so

empty—

so

how

can

we

tell

what's

inside

us?

Would

anyone

Listen?

Would

anyone

care?

Would

everyone

Runaway?

And

then

where

would

we

be?

Can

anyone

know

how

it

hurts

so

inside?

Does

anything

show?

And

if

they

were

to

listen,

if

they

were

to

see,

would

they

ever

be

able

to

Love

Us—

Would

they

ever

Love

Me?

Hear

Me?

See

Me?

Cry

for

Me?

Can

I

really

be———

o.k.?

I want to be a house with windows open to the sun

I

want

to

be

a

house

with

windows

open

to

the

Sun.

Furniture

arranged,

in

place,

comfortable

and

overstuffed

with

dreams.

Free

from

tears,

or

shredded

pillows

in

slanted

colors:

Frayed

secrets,

tattered

and

turned

inward;

past

moments

scattered

in

the

frame

like

sand

in

a

wound.

If

I

could

be

a

house

filled

with

Sunlight,

measuring

the

hours

in

time

with

the

turning

Earth.

Not

out

of

season,

too

hot,

too

cold.

Not

harboring

entrances

to

empty

rooms

or

doors

that

will

not

open.

If

I

could

be

free

to

walk

through

the

corridors

of

my

self

and

rest

anywhere,

at

any

moment:

If

I

could

just

turn

the

key

and

be

Home.

If I can be somebody

If

I

can

be

in

somebody's

heart,

somebody's

eye,

somebody's

mind.

If

I

can

be

not

dirty,

or

ugly,

or

small,

or

bad.

If

I

can

be

like

a

leaf

in

the

wind,

or

green

grass,

facing

the

sky,

or

a

song

carried

by

the

breeze.

Let

me

be

beautiful

in

somebody's

eye.

Let

me

be

able

to

look

at

myself

and

say,

"How

wonderful

that

God

stopped

by

to

make

me."

I get so angry

I

get

so

angry

at

myself,

sometimes.

It's

as

if

I

can't

really

put

my

anger

Anyplace

else.

Nobody

listens

to

the

song

of

pain

I

sing.

Nobody

knows

how

sad

I

can

be come.

My

anger

shouts

with

a

Loud

voice.

Hits

with

a

tough

Fist.

And

I

slam

at

others,

but

mostly,

at

myself:

dirty

ugly

stupid

Bad.

Sometimes

I

hurt

myself

so

that

I

can

command

my

pain.

I

am

the

general,

the

power,

the

conquerer.

Even

if

the

only

victim

is

me.

That's

the

loneliest

time:

All

alone

like

a

Burning

star,

Shining

in

the

dark.

Yearning

to

be

free.

ACTIVITIES FOR PART III:
FEELING OUT OF PLACE

So me times I feel so out of step
I want to be somebody from somewhere
Sometimes it's hard to just keep on going
Sometimes I feel like a dog who quacks
Can anyone see?
I want to be a house with windows open to the sun
If I can be somebody
I get so angry

- What are all of the different feelings you've had in the past week? Write out all the letters of the alphabet, A to Z. Think of a word that describes how you've felt for each of the letters of the alphabet. For example, "angry" for A, "babyish" for B, "capable" for C, and so on.

- Think about something that someone said to you that either made you feel really good about yourself or something that really hurt your feelings. Start your poem with what that person said, then write about how it made you feel. For example, your poem might start, "My teacher said to me, 'Sandy, you can always make me smile!' and immediately I felt…"

- Keep thinking about what that person said to you. Write a pretend letter to that person—a letter that you're not going to deliver. Tell them how they made you feel and why.

- Write a poem that starts, "When I feel angry, it's because…"

- Pick an emotion. Make a list of 5 things that make you feel that emotion. Your list is a poem!

- Have you ever had a day when everything that could have gone wrong went wrong? Imagine that you could live that day over again. Write a poem or story about how you could change that day.

- Do you sometimes wish that you were already grown up? If you magically were an adult for a day, how would you act? Imagine if you were the teacher of your class for a day. What would you teach? Write a story about what would happen if you were an adult for a day.

- Life doesn't always make sense. Write a poem that is only made up of questions.

- Draw a totally new monster—one that's never been drawn before. Write a poem about that monster. What does it look like? Smell like? What does it do for fun?

- If love was a color, what color would it be? What color is happiness? What color is fear? What color is excitement? Take a poem that you've already written, about feelings or emotions—or write a new one! Find colored markers or crayons. Rewrite your poem, but every time you write a word that is about an emotion, write it in the color of that emotion.

PART IV:
POSITIVE FEELINGS

I am special

I

am

special

because

I

Am.

One day

One

day,

walking

down

my

mind,

looking

for

places

to

sit

and

rest,

feeling

alone

and

not

very

special,

I

encountered

the

idea

that

I

am

Somebody.

All

by

myself.

Really.

Somebody.

And

I

looked

around

for

somebody

else

to

affirm

this

new

Truth,

But

there

was

nobody

there.

Just

me.

Just

Me.

So

I

sat

there

quietly

in

the

center

of

myself

and

watched

the

colors

of

my

dreams

as

they

floated

by.

I am unique in All creation

I

own

what

I

think

and

what

I

write

upon

a

page.

No one

can

think

exactly

like

I

do.

I

am

unique

in

All

creation.

I love my body

I love my

body.

It's

so

Cool.

I can

Wiggle

my

toes.

I can

Cross

my

eyes.

I

can

Make

my

lips

look

really

Ugly—

like a

 jelly

fish.

I

can

Skip

and

Run

and

Feel

the

sand

and

the

Foamy

waves

on

my

legs

and

hands

and

feet—

It's sweet

Being

me,

with

Everything

I

can

feel

and

see.

And

all

my

Parts

work

just

for

me!

I

own

this

Place.

I

am

the

Sole

owner

of

the

Universe

of

Me!

Wow!

So

listen

self:

Thank you,

Brain.

Thank you,

Heart.

Thank you,

Legs.

Thank you,

Fingers.

Thank you,

Toes.

Thank you,

Interesting parts

mostly

covered

by

clothes.

I

am

giving

you

all

a

raise

and

a

bonus.

I

Declare

this

day

The

Day

Of

Me!

A

Holiday!

A

Celebration!

For

all

of

the

Parts

of

the

M E

nation.

Applause

to

my

Lips

my

Hips

my

Nose

my

Ears

my

Chin

my

Knees

my

Toes.

Take the day off!

Go out!

Stay in!

Celebrate

the

glorious

fabulous

Shape

that

you're

in.

I am a candle in the light of myself

I

am

a

candle

in

the

light

of

my

self.

I

falter,

sometimes,

and

it

looks

like

I

am

going

to

sputter

and

die.

But

I

will

not

Ex

Tin

Guish.

I

will

not

go

out.

I

will

continue

to

light

my

own

way.

Terror

en

gulfs

me

like

a

great

tsunami.

But

I

will

not

die:

From

the

darkness,

I

will

add

my

luminosity

to

the

Light

of

the

world.

I should count for something

I

should

count

for

something.

My

being

should

count

for

something.

My

being

here

should

count

for

Something.

Don't

let

me

be

nothing.

nobody.

Even

space

between

objects—

no

matter

how

far

a

part—

is

something.

All the Power Rests with You

You belong to yourself.

Celebrate the things that belong to you.

Nobody can take away from you what belongs to you.

Clap your hands!

Stamp your feet!

Stretch your arms out as far as they can go,

And Dance.

Now dance in a circle.

Hug yourself.

Touch your nose.

Touch your toes.

Touch your ears.

Wiggle your eyebrows.

Make funny faces.

Make funny voices.

And Smile—the biggest smile you can!

Write a poem about your smile.

Write a poem about your toes.

Write a poem about your nose.

Think about all who love you.

The sky loves you.

The trees love you.

The rocks love you.

Even the bugs that scamper and get away from the stamp of your feet

Love you.

l

Love you.

God loves you.

Write some poems about the things who love you.

Write a poem about the sky.

Write a poem about a flower.

Write a poem about a tree.

Write a poem about the sea.

Now write a poem about yourself.

Sometimes things hurt you.

People can hurt you.

Things that happen can make you feel sad inside.

Write a poem about what hurts you.

Write a poem about what makes you sad.

And then REMEMBER to STAMP your feet,

And touch your ears

And touch your toes

And hug yourself with a very big smile.

Because!!!!!

Only you belong to you.

What's missing? Sometimes tears are missing.

When we cry we water the sky.

Tears make things grow.

Sometimes, they make us grow inside, because they tell us how we feel.

They are our way of talking to ourselves, sometimes.

All of us feel sorry, when we are sad.

Sometimes, tears are necessary to let us know that it's o.k. to feel sad sometimes.

Think of your favorite colors.

Write your colors.

Write a poem about each of your favorite colors.

The world is made up of beautiful things.

You are one of the world's beautiful things.

Close your eyes. What colors do you see?

Open your eyes. What colors do you see?

Think of sounds.

Some sounds are good sounds.

Name the good sounds.

Name the bad sounds.

Write about the good sounds.

Write about the bad sounds.

What feels good?

Write about what feels good.

Write about what feels bad.

Remember. You belong to you.

You will always belong to you.

You will always have a friend.

Because you are your own friend.

You are your own, very own, very own, best friend.

Anything you say to you is o.k.

Anything you feel inside you is o.k.

You can love you, and love you and love you—as much as you want.

You belong to you, always and forever.

Think about babies.

Think about

New things

Small things

True things

Safe things.

Think about butterfly wings.

All the world belongs to you.

All the world belongs to you.

Believe this and you make it true.

All the power rests with you.

Touch your feelings.

How far do they go?

Can you touch them like you touch your nose?

Do they stop at the end of your toes?

What makes you happy?

What makes you sad?

What makes you angry?

What makes you care?

What do you care about?

How rich you are!

How rich you are!

You own your eyes,

Your nose

Your ears

Your toes

Your hands

Your feet

Your smile

Your teeth!

You own all that you see and feel.

And if you feel it, then it's real.

You own the sky above your head.

You own the dreams you have at night.

You own the thoughts that sing inside.

You own the love that holds you tight.

You own tomorrow and today

And all the love that comes your way.

ALL THE POWER RESTS WITH YOU.

ACTIVITIES FOR PART IV:
POSITIVE FEELINGS

I am special
One day
I am unique in All creation
I love my body
I am a candle in the light of myself
I should count for something
All the Power Rests with You

- Write a poem about all the new things you've learned to do in the past year.

- If you could have the power of a special super hero, who would you choose? Write a story or a poem about how you would use your new power.

- Write your name out backwards. Sarah Hunt is "Haras Tnuh." This is the name of a new character who is opposite from you in every way. Write a story about that character.

- Who is your real life hero? Write a poem or a story that explains why your hero is great.

- Think of a quote that you really like, either from a famous person or from someone you know. Write a story or poem that begins with that quote.

- Who is your favorite character in your favorite movie, book, or tv show? Imagine if one day you switched places with that character. How would you live that character's life for a day? Write a story or a poem about it.

- Write out all the letters of your name. Write a positive word that describes you for each letter. For example, "athletic" for A, "brainy" for B, or "creative" for C.

PART V:
THE FUTURE

Star-Moon in the night

Star-

moon,

in

the

night,

looking

down

on

me,

how

I

wish

that

I

could

light

my

world.

I

wish

I

could

I

wish

I

might

have

the

wish

I

make

tonight.

Please

make

the

pain

go

all

away.

Please

make

Somebody

love

me.

Pray

that

all

my

days

be

bright,

and

that

I

make

another

night.

Wish

on

me,

and

I

on

you

that

all

our

wishes

will

come

True.

This I tell you

This

I

tell

you,

my

darlings,

because

I

love

you

so

much:

Life

is

not

black

or

white,

but

all

the

colors

in

between.

You

are

not

good,

or

bad,

but

a

combination

of

many

actions,

and

even,

dreams.

We

are

made

each

of

us

different,

recognized

for

the

beauty

of

our

im

per

fec

tions.

I

know

this,

because

I

am

old.

Life

has

told

me,

great

Teacher

that

she

is,

to

be

patient

with

myself,

to

look

over

the

stars

at

the

far

Universe,

and

to

blow

kisses

to

each

shadow

I

reflect

as

I

change

into

a

new

being.

So

I

tell

you,

Children,

because

I

have

seen

the

angels

smiling

in

the

dark,

that

everything

is

indeed

O.

K.

That

you

are

a

piece

of

the

wondrous

Spark

of

life.

Imperfectly-

perfect—

in

every

way.

Who am I?

Sometimes

I

feel

so

alone

and

afraid.

How

can

I

go

another

day?

Who

can

I

tell

my

troubles

to?

Who

will

listen?

Who

will

love

me?

Who

will

stand

by

my

side?

I

just

want

to

hide.

How

can

I

know

what

to

do?

At

such

times,

if

I

listen

deeply

to

the

voice

with in

my

self,

It

will

tell

me

the

answers,

and

show

me

the

way.

It

will

say:

I

am

today.

I

am

the

morning

sun,

the

rain

as

it

mists

the

trees.

I

am

the

evening

storm.

I

am

the

breeze

that

shakes

the

flowers'

leaves

and

moves

the

fur

upon

the

Great

giraffe

as

he

flutters

his

round

dark

eyes

at

Life.

I

am

Everyone

who

came

before

me,

loving

and

cheering

me

forward

as

.

only

Ancestors

can,

knowing

that

anger

and

bitterness

and

war

and

betrayal

mean

Nothing

over

Time.

I

stand

today

for

This

moment.

I

Am

this

moment,

standing,

poised

between

now

and

the

next

Beginning,

which

I

hold

in

the

Blink

of

my

eyes,

the

beat

of

my

heart,

the

song

of

my

Soul.

I

am

today.

But

I

am

also

tomorrow.

I

am

all

that

was,

and

all

that

will

Be.

ACTIVITIES FOR PART V:
THE FUTURE

Star-Moon in the night

- What do you wish for? Write a poem that's all about your hopes and wishes. You can start each line with, "I wish," or "I hope."

This I tell you

- You're a much different person than you were 5 years ago. Imagine what you'll be like 50 years from now! Where will you live? Who will you live with? What will you look like? What will you enjoy doing? Write down 10 things that you hope you'll remember about being a kid.

- Imagine you are 50 years older than you are now. As an adult, write a letter to your childhood self. What would you want to say?

Who am I?

- Start writing about who you are, where you come from, what you want, and what you plan to do in life. You can write anything you want, because you know all about who you are and where you come from—and even what you want—for what is important to you IS important. What do you think you would like to be? How would you like to spend your life? What are your dreams and hopes for the future?

Remember that what you say and what you think and who you are is important. You are somebody special, just because you're you.

About the Author

Dr. Suzanne Stutman is a Professor of English, American Studies, and Women's Studies at Penn State University's Abington College. She is the author of five scholarly texts and three books of poetry: *Broken Feather: A Journey to Healing, White Feather: A Journey to Peace, and All the Power Rests with You.* Dr. Stutman has written poetry on behalf of several organizations, including The International Health Awareness Network, The National Council of Women of the United States, The International Council of Women, Friends of the Children (The Center for Children's Support), The Philadelphia Children's Alliance, Women Organized Against Rape, and Heartbeat, South Africa. Her poems have been read and exhibited at the United Nations and at various locations around the world.

Dr. Stutman is the Immediate Past President of the National Council of Women of the United States and Vice President of Educational Outreach for the International Health Awareness Network. She is also a past president of The Thomas Wolfe Society. She serves on the advisory boards of the Toni Morrison Society, The Thomas Wolfe Society, and the Survivors' Art Foundation.

BOOK PRODUCTION

Cover Design: Geralynne Slowe
Graphic Design: Alex Shin
Printer: McNaughton & Gunn, Inc.

A portion of the proceeds from the sale of this book will be
donated to the following child protection agencies:
The Philadelphia Children's Alliance
Heartbeat, South Africa
WOAR— Counseling for Children and Teens
The International Health Awareness Network

Manor House Publications, Inc.
3501 Newberry Road
Philadelphia, PA 19154
800-343-8464
manorhousepublications.com
peace-healingbooks.com